POEMS

LAUREN

BRAZEAL

YESYES
BOOKS

Her

GUTTER

© 2018 BY LAUREN BRAZEAL

COVER ART: "GUTTER" WITH PERMISSION FROM THOMPSON REUTERS

COVER AND INTERIOR DESIGN: ALBAN FISCHER

PRINTED IN THE UNITED STATES OF AMERICA

PUBLISHED BY YESYES BOOKS

1614 NE ALBERTA ST

PORTLAND, OR 97211

YESYESBOOKS.COM

KMA SULLIVAN, PUBLISHER

JOANN BALINGIT, ASSISTANT EDITOR

STEVIE EDWARDS, SENIOR EDITOR, BOOK DEVELOPMENT

ALBAN FISCHER, GRAPHIC DESIGNER

COLE HILDEBRAND, SENIOR EDITOR OF OPERATIONS

JILL KOLONGOWSKI, MANAGING EDITOR

BEYZA OZER, DEPUTY DIRECTOR OF SOCIAL MEDIA

AMBER RAMBHAROSE, CREATIVE DIRECTOR OF SOCIAL MEDIA

CARLY SCHWEPPE, ASSISTANT EDITOR, *VINYL*

LEVI TODD, ASSISTANT EDITOR, *VINYL*

PHILLIP B. WILLIAMS, COEDITOR IN CHIEF, *VINYL*

AMIE ZIMMERMAN, EVENTS COORDINATOR

HARI ZIYAD, ASSISTANT EDITOR, *VINYL*

For those who were there

*Confession is always weakness. The grave soul keeps its own secrets, and takes its own punishment in silence.*

—DOROTHY DIX

# CONTENTS

## MOUSE,

I need to speak to you        in the present tense.

You're leaning towards me so I know you're listening.

Your mohawk has grown out, your boots held together by pins.

I touch your delicate fingers with my mouth

and swallow them

to have parts of you I can carry.

I need language only we can understand.


Can you remember kneeling in the field, flames everywhere?

People scream at the fire because they don't know what it is


—they haven't learned to sleep in it.


Imagine the beginning:

I spy you slouched in mid-day shadow.        Palm trees rush like cilia around us.

I ask for a cigarette.

We both have black-eyes.

I kissed you because we both had black-eyes.

# ROBBY TOOK BETS TO SEE
# WHEN I'D GET OFF MY HIGH HORSE
# AND START EATING TRASH

Seasoned workers
      would have spent all night
on this display.

It's Christmas
      at the mall.
Windows glisten.

Cookie cutter
      doll boy angels,
swathed in caramel-

colored coats
      of butter soft satin,
spiral

from the ceilings
      of the halls, like ham
salting on twine.

Hand tossed & glazed
      mint-tangerine
tea sets sweetly

offer to toast

  the newest year

near Macy's.


Little girl

  mannequins cinnamon twirl

in every children's wing.


See how life-

  like they look. They flaunt

their fullness,


and I want them

  all, trussed and boiling

in a fat black pot.


Outside, it's colder.

  Plum-violet mountains

pinch a mouth


from the sugarless horizon.

  Snowcaps sharpen into teeth.

Wicked is the throat, the tongue.


Wicked are the eyes.

# GIRL TWO WAYS,
# FOR MR. BLACK

**1.** *Gobbler Nymphette:*

Fourteen        friendless        classified

      as cricket-thighed
          and nickel-tittied, I stripped meadows of their petals.

Those jealous witches
      in fifth period never bought I'd met an older man.

To test my honesty, they taught
      me how to slice delirious
black hearts into the paper after every declaration,
      They didn't teach me how to beg.

          I knew to pray:
              *Please please please*
      *unsheathe and find me thick*
        *enough to take in each new penetration.*

      *Love me with your handle, open palmed.*
*Love me with your mouth, the blade.*

Convinced I had a choice,     I chose serrations

                    in the teeth:     those pink

            striated devastations.


I ♥ I ♥ your kisses sugar-laced,


     every gift-horse laceration.


## 2. *Saintly Double Fisted:*


     Then the desert blistered around us.

Sun-hot bones traced           fissures in mud           your words

     *all this was ocean once.*


Mesas knifed into view.

     Each night's ruin cleaved

          another scapula-wedged moon.


The bus we caught ant-trailed the continent

     to an intended


     destination. Your hands shut on mine like a prayer-book.


*Learn to beg,*

          you said, *to suffer is conditional of suffering.*

O never

        leave me lonesome      fawn-lipped horizon

    broad-edged rock

half-gone husk of a dog.

# ABOUT THE PLACES
## WHERE WE SLEPT

We called them
home, honed

in on them, nestled
like hornets, or nested

horned pit vipers.
We filed

into them from streets,
filled out

their gauntness
stretched our limbs

within them, clamored
climbed. The squat

is action: to keep
anonymous by way

of crouch; or object
space now occupied

7

a sequestering place.
To be squatting

is simply holding
onto, or having held

illegally, taken
shelter in, to shill

as never settled
any *where* shuttered

and left empty.
Without fuss,

we set up shop
made our beds

tidy, then bed down
until up-

rooted, turned out,
cast away like jetsam,

jettisoned.
We of *find* and *hide*,

always found
and hounded; we

the landless,

faceless, walless,

roofless,
groundless ones

always called them home
if asked.

| | | | | |
|---|---|---|---|---|
| Anti-abortionist "soup" | Not-so-orange chicken from the dumpster at P.F. Chang's | Hari Krishna lotus chips after a lecture on abstaining from pollutant foods | Take from the take-out window at California Pizza Kitchen | Sleep for dinner |
| Share a garbage bag of soggy popcorn from behind the movie theater | Sleep for dinner | Attend to unattended food court kiosks at the mall | Beg for change, get spat on, make a buck in nickels | Shoplift candy one more time from the pharmacy on 5th |
| Sleep for dinner | Beg for change, get told to find a job, make a buck in pennies | Free Meal ☺ | Sleep for dinner | Clotted chocolate clumps from the dumpster at The Fudgeworks |
| Grab and dash a sample plate from the food court at the mall | Trimmings from behind the Brazilian steak house | Sleep for dinner | Mostly eaten "New York" slices from the trash | Cold french fries from patio tables on the pier (get there before the birds do) |
| Cheese? From the dumpster at the tapas bar | Sleep for dinner | Beg for doggie bags from bitches on the promenade | Month old veggies from behind the Taco Mucho | Crash & Stash at a 7-11 |

veins that steel blossomed
barrel tightens your hand
on my jaw smooths your
fist down my spine's teeth
shift the splintered ground
around me folds so there
is no one to hear us only
you needle your elbow into
my ribs cave both lungs
compress when you finger
my tongue fluid forces air
from the barrel slides the
hammer back plunges my
chin into your collar bones
and skin and bones and
skin and bones hollow my
stomach when you promise
no one will find what's left of
me being smaller than you
grow on top you animal growl
be still but it's hard with so
much blood in my mouth

# THE WITCH/MENDER

We found her in The Diggs.

Known for reading
> fortune-telling bones,
>> she collected dirty female
>>> charms—doll legs
>>> and seagull eggshells.

I was carried to her once
> the sun sank
> because the bleeding hadn't stopped.

An art exists
whereby a vase or bowl,
once shattered, is repaired
with solid gold;
> this action illuminates impermanence: the zen of fracture

>> —a warlord dreamed it up.

In the blind sockets of those cliffs, she sealed
me with a spool of light-

absorbing fishing line and clear-dry crazy glue.

We needed to conceal the injury.


Weakness glints,

luring tertiary predators.

# WE WROTE VILLANELLES AT THE SUNRISE GROUP HOME FOR WAYWARD TEENS

No need to suck a cock when I can steal
supplies to last a couple days. It's time
      to find a weapon loud enough to speak.

I loved that Go-Go Gadget as a kid at Grandma's house.
Here, home becomes a place to sleep mouth open.
      No need to rent mine out when I can find

a corner of my own to doze in. No one bothers tossing worries
at a skeevy punk gone missing—no green pennies rusting in my fountain.
      I'll equip a weapon sharper than my tongue

maybe hitch a ride to Crescent City, string a hammock one mile up
in all those voiceless trees; their creaks, the only sounds I want to hear.
      No need to suck a cock. Now I can dream

more vividly when a neck knife guards the zipper to my jeans, and bubblegum
wrapped razor blades nest between my lips and teeth.
      Weaponize all things around me, no more begging

*please* and *don't.* My street witch mother taught me all that separates a house
and alley cat: only one will share a kill with those who might betray it.
      No need to suck on cocks, or anything but lollipops. I'll wield
      a diesel-powered set of lungs to rip the voice of man clean out.

# L.A. PASTORAL
## (WRITTEN IN SHARPIE ON A
## BATHROOM WALL IN SANTA MONICA)

Before each sunrise

the city gathers kelp knots

      clearing jogging paths.

Our absence of faith

in nature to self-govern

      creates this buzzing.

      Unable to run

a comb through my own wild locks,

I razor them off.

*Fig 1. Cut out and tuck in belt for emergencies*

# DEAR FATHER (SHOPPING WITH YOUR FAMILY OF FOUR ON A SATURDAY NIGHT ON 3RD ST, PRETENDING NOT TO STARE)

You look at me
because you're sizing me up,
because I'm clothes on bones,

because you wonder
what I smell like naked.
I have a gun

I don't know how to use,
a pair of pliers, two shoes, a bag of jewel cases.
I have a lean red hound waking in my stomach.

I have memories of things
that never happened, or you offered
a dollar to swallow your cock.

You're naming me in this moment.
I answer to Casualty
and Lost. I answer to Whore,

Corpse, Ghost.
You've labeled me Victim.
You'll label me Cunt.

But would you call me Darling?
Could you call me Daughter
if you liked?

You look away
but my blood-skinned
hound has eyed you.

I, too, judge what I see
and the hunter within me
is stalking.

# BUT, MR. BLACK,

it wasn't a dream. Animals ate
the flesh of lesser animals
    until we swam a frenzied
sea of drippings,
       then were raked
    and fashioned into brand new selves
of gristle, tooth, and clot.


Foraging was always
    just a piece of our survival.


I see you still
    plucking the legs off that beetle.
    It tried to fly
    but the body
could only bat and scratch
    against the tiles. You say cruelty
  is an abstraction.


    If you'd trapped it in your mouth
you would have felt
    its wings flick against your teeth.
  By biting down
      you could have kept
    even that sound from escaping.

# CAN CART MAN

Luck keeps him clanking from a block away, his carts refilled
with cans and other gleaming trinkets. Everything rejected

by the ocean ends up as his stock: shark-fins, bits
of a Ukrainian fishing boat, broke up sea glass round

as junkie eyes. Sometimes he'll catch a purse of kittens
and sell them for sweet tobacco, from which he twists

his fragile, knobby cigarettes. Then we'll have a party, maybe
some Kentucky whiskey. Every day he asks that God forgive

this thirsty sin and will admit he dwells on carnal pleasure. No good
rain in Southern California means he's slow to shower in the sea. He'll crack

salt chips straight from his hair, our can cart man, who is unique
because he's ours. He matters in this way.

I'll always cherish your floor: cold red tiles in the morning. Your glass storefronts poised to shriek if a brick's thrown through them. They guard the Swarovski, Valentino, Prada and Chanel I wait to steal until the sun smirks, high and defiant; when shop girls file their nails and ignore my slithering through their aisles. I sell my score in your double-jawed parking structure, stalked by Malibu teenagers who'd rather get what things they want for just enough to buy a burger. Starvation unifies, friend maker. Thanks for offering your putrefied Lobster Putanesca and Fiesta Rigatoni that I slide into my stomach, your patio tables obscuring my shadow, your pocketable cutlery. Thanks for all the manicured dinosaur statues, those half empty wine bottles, the sheltering alleys, your ashtrays overflowing with succulent butts.

XOXOXO,

Little Mohawked Squatter Punk

21

## GROWING UP IS LOSING SOME ILLUSIONS IN ORDER TO ACQUIRE OTHERS

A stolen *Popular*
*Science* magazine explains

rodent and dog retinas
favor nighttime vision

over color:
scavengers just need

two tones to know
what's *kill*,

*forage*, or *flee*.
Mouse, you and I believe

that will can triumph
over nature,

and graffiti lime,
magenta, puce

on every overpass and wall
(beauty's measured

now through size
and difficulty to erase).

We refuse to turpentine
our vivid desolation.

Comfort me.
Or just don't look at this

collapsing
scratch-n-scream expanse

of loss and foam
and wind—and please

stop saying
that we're weak.

Tell me, instead, why stars
wield names like *Gladys,*

and pollution
from the east meanders

down to Venice Beach,
like a pack of sheep.

You openly lament
about commuters

missing out
on all the scenery,

and I remember
hearing, once, this smog

intensifies the colors
of our sunsets.

# JEAN GENET
## REINCARNATES AS A PIG

Now I don't expect

what's coming from the world.

That's part of the appeal, I'm sure.

My kin—my co-conspirators and I—

live snout to ass in icy shit, hoping

there's a field beyond the chutes and corners,

always an out before the ax,

where sections of the floor suddenly slide back,

sending all of us cartwheeling

onto fattened mattresses, greased with endless hay

and slop and sex until, exhausted,

we resign to twitch limbs in our slumber

to keep the flies from landing.

Humans, when they choose

to view us, drive home traumatized.

25

# HOW TO CAPTURE THE ESCAPING MAN
## (FOUND CAREFULLY FOLDED IN
### AN ARMY SURPLUS BACKPACK)

Note:

• Even flashing lights refuse to pulse in stills

• Lead, triggers, fenced-off fields around the road will give you gray

• Teeth and cigarettes remain allusions to a rapidly approaching danger

| Step 1: |
|---|
| Illuminate his chewed up hair, the absent clenching jaw he executes; the mind, a wilderness of feral thoughts. It helps to fabricate some memories of sun-blind rabbits flushed by eager hounds. |
| Step 2: |
| Reveal his body only through the shadows bearing it. Don't reward the thing from which he flees; keep it always almost upon him. |

Addendum to Note:

xi. Black is blood

xii. Exposed eye whites are animal

xiii. If everything could be immovable

| 4. ~~Cut the gun from his lap.~~ |
|---|
| 5. Frame him so the edges sever his elbows, hips, and knees. |
| 6. Undo his bindings or he'll never be yours. |

Just close your eyes and shoot.

# IF EVER ASKED TO DESCRIBE ALL IT WAS (WRITTEN ON A PALIMPSEST OF TRUMAN CAPOTE'S *IN COLD BLOOD*)

LA, too, can be seen from great distances. Not that there is much to see—simply an aimless congregation of warehouses, boutiques, and liquor stores, divided in the center by [] the poor and the rich; fed by a supply of pilgrims. [] After seasonal winds, or when the streets, all unnamed, all unshaded, all unpaved, are cleaned and left sparkling, person-faced silhouettes appear in dirty doorways, stairwells, and alleys. Visibility relies on contrast. At one end of the town sags an old hill pretending to be a mountain, the crest of which supports a raggedy cut-out sign--"HOLLYWOOD"— Nearby in a [] building, another sign with an irrelevant warning [] reads in flaking gold on the scummiest window--"NO Cameras." [] the majority of LA's homes are tucked behind walls, outfitted with locks, passcodes, and panic rooms.

# ANOTHER THING
## ABOUT MR. BLACK

I need to share the story
        so I won't be alone with it:
his hand Debt Collector took
        a hammer to in Hollywood.

Doctors would have hacked it off
            at the wrist, or smothered
it in plaster, but, neglected, those bones fused
counter-clockwise in knots,
the flesh boiled over at the knuckles,
              and the thing grew
      heavy as a grudge.

          I hate the way it curled into itself
as if cold, and begged
for attention like a guilt-inducing memory.

I hate that weaknesses demand compassion.

       —Though I'll admit,
at night, asleep, it acted
almost innocent: those once beloved
fingers shuddered back to life,
        revived as twitching whiskers

             feeling out a dream.

28

# WITH ROBBY: WHITE HOUSE, GRAY SHUTTERS, ROSEBUSH

I stop to admire the sinkful of plates

the dish of cat food

beside a dish of water.

A blue-checked towel hangs on a hook

beside a slender vase for flowers.

A clock ticks in another room.

Robby brushes past me

with a stereo and I roll open

drawers lined with cutlery

then move onto the cupboards.

Now my eyes organize

rows of cans, finding what should be carried

in the dark: two tins of salmon

the sack of apples, not the onion

not the artichokes, the box of breakfast cereal

not the bowls; in the den

the fat book of CDs

to be stripped and fenced.

Not the little girl's room.

I'll take the slick

loops of pearls, not the pill-shaped

pillows on the bed.

I check the silver for stamps

as he taught me many houses ago.

From the window, I watch him slip

between the hedges. Now I am alone.
The space becomes so still, I can feel dust
settle on my eyelashes. I light a cigarette
and burn my name into the air.

# LITTLE MOHAWKED SQUATTER PUNK
## CONFRONTS THE MOON

Asshat Romans swore you blessed their hunts.
You've put on quite a show but we've cooked up
our own hi-tech mythology: fluorescent
words that sear instead of glow. I'm sick
of your kimonoed kissy-cunt routine.
That cute mute sheen of yours illuminates
your laughable pudenda. You'd bleed out
in any fight with us muck dwellers, coiled
in fetal pose: a bawling lotus. We
replaced your fuck-faced face with freeway lamps
and no one noticed. So you LOL
and wink at puddles? Justify your place,
you pussy bitch, when new muses exist:
goliaths pieced from cocks, fast cars, and shit.

A coil's popped

       in my jaw and half

my face unhinges when I talk. What keeps this skull

      moored to these shoulders also apes


      a bobbleheaded doll.

            My pelvis clacks: froggy

    and flat, but my body's longer

      edge-winged ends have

hollow points. Other girls in line count pocks

      in clouds and kick

    loose asphalt chunks

by sunshine-ripened piss on sidewalks.


I've finally arrived:

      receptive as a pipe.



      Toss a pen, insult, glass eye, or flashlight down


        one end of me and watch it fly,

unaltered, out the other side.

# WHAT WE SEE
# WHAT WE WANT TO SEE

but he wouldn't take the name we gave him first. Wanted to earn respect the way a rich boy does: he tried to buy it with cigarettes and weed. We didn't waste time on him, but he kept hanging around, laughing too loud, lighting farts, muscling in on squats. The idiot didn't know how to make himself invisible. Enter Rubia: I saw her eyes narrow from a block away when he flashed his leather jacket. She'd shaved her head fresh with a turquoise mohawk and laced her arms from wrist to elbow with fake gold bangles. All she had to do was grab my wrist and give me a look, and we asked him to come with us to see the beach—*like a threesome.* We took him through a garage near the elevators and got him in the emergency stairwell. My hands trembled. I threw a shopping bag over his head and Rubia cracked his knees, doubling him over. (No one squatted without a smiley or something heavy worth swinging). We hit his face with a brick until blood finally flowered under the plastic and he slumped over, then I rolled him out of his coat and gave it to her. I knew the meaning of what we'd done. That's how I remember it now: the blossoms beneath the bag exploding like watercolors. They reminded me of when I was a kid on some field trip away from home and we went to a museum which paired poems with old paintings. There was this one mural with red fireworks reflected off a lake beside a temple. I heard the kid wound up in the ICU. At night sometimes I'd jolt awake, breathless, and see nothing until my eyes finally zeroed in on the pink-black sky's polluted, open mouth. I wanted to believe the city was a big oyster: pearls everywhere, and we never thought twice about taking anything we needed. Our minds became our reactions to actions: just a long hallway lined with closed doors, ringing in their locks. I never saw Rubia in that jacket, not even once. Last I heard she hopped a train to Seattle.

Whispers of your HIV
       spread
from the sex
          pits in West Hollywood
and killed all dreams
             of any lasting freedom.

You should have legged it, lit out to what freedom
         could be stolen. How do you outrun HIV?
(In my dreams,
           I was able to stop its spread
by unrolling myself over Hollywood
             like a condom). Pimps keep their sex

stalls primped with fresh-from-prairie stock, but there's no sex
         ed. for bottom bitches. *Miss T will you clench our freedom?*
*Get ourselves a Hollywood*
           *Love Story, with dancing, songs, and kisses in Times Square?*—your HIV
kept me from asking. Talk spread:
           the bug was crawling, and your dreams

—mostly fever dreams
       of choking, sticky-money sex,
retching by lit candles—overtook you. I couldn't spread
         a parachute or conjure freedom,

batter your HIV

        with medicine, shoot Hollywood's

square eyes a glance. I couldn't hold a gun to anything in Hollywood.
      Unruly dreams
were suffocated for us. HIV
        dictated: any woman pinched and labeled *sex*
*worker* got handed a felony. Miss T, you traded freedom
          in the squatter's racket for a slim-fit rut on which to perch spread-

eagle, spread
      your heart's wide open arms for Hollywood,
and were toppled for it. No freedom
        rings in a cell door's echo at sundown: where dreams

house the only wind some ever feel again. Sex
         is what you had, and your dying years locked up with HIV.

You grew to think of HIV—and even AIDS—as a kind of freedom.
      Everybody's dreams spread latex thin, stained by sex
like badly tattooed skin. Hushed endings find too many here in Hollywood.

# CRADLE SONG FOR THE GIRL
## NOT YET HOMELESS

Each night I'm tucked

           in under assembled tar and shingles. Naked

Barbies, taped into their polyester

           cherry coverlets, rest at every angle

so that all of them can fit

           inside the Dream

House®. At 2am

           my father crunches

numbers at a folding table.

           My mother starts to take

on extra work, which means more time away from us.

           I've learned

the proper place for everything.

           Raccoons and deer hide

in a forest. Bad guys

           go to jail. Lions sleep

in cages at the zoo.

           By day, kneeling in the street,

           I'm sketching angels

on the pavement—it's August

           and my aunt has died.

I surround her form unsteadily

           with wings and make her

smile, so everyone can see it.

           She must be happy now:

finally re-housed

        among God's chosen. *Free*

*of suffering,* my mother

        says. I'm told to gift her

with a halo or else

        she ends up homeless:

*just a ghost.*

        Darkness everlasting

hinges on the details.

# TO JENNIFER LOVE-HEWITT:
## I SAW YOU AT FENDI LAST WEEK—
## I WAS THE LITTLE MOHAWKED
## SQUATTER PUNK PANHANDLER

TRANSMITTED VIA FACSIMILE

RE: Los Angeles County case #24789. Letter was balled up and tied to a padlock, found thrown through the southernmost window at Love-Hewitt estate. <u>Status: Unsolved</u>

Dear Jenny,

        If I had real access
to the internet I'd follow       and unfollow and refollow you
on twitter,      proving how relentless I can be and

        I'd unfriend you every night
    on facebook
so you'd wake up
    every corresponding morning
to my sweet smile widening
      your friend requests.

I'd celebrate each homecoming as though it was my first.

        Oh Jen, you'd ache
and love    and keep
my slender hands wrist-deep inside you, cradling

your weaker structures. Forget forever
how us girls evolved to cake

      foundation on unsightly ruptures. Never beg
for mercy from a man again;
curl your toes for my forgiving      tongue instead and crack
a little extra space
        between those legs.

     I'd rip you
from that pretty red Moschino dress,
and hook your thorax on a pin     to keep you
splayed     and still, and posed for action;
like a vulva-colored lady praying
mantis—     I'll show you other flower-mimic
predators we mutually
     relate to if you let me in

to this big terra-cotta
     house of yours. What did it cost you?

       I bet, combined,
our scars would trace God's very spine.
It makes me sick how pitch
     perfectly alike we are: both of us women
—teenyboppers really—
    making origami
of our sex to serve a world drunk,
      guzzling fragility.

Though you're the one they think about
when they're settling for me.


You stuck-up bitch I'd love
to show you how it feels
                to withstand hypodermic teeth;
        be overlooked, replaceable,
dangling just inside the serpent's reach.        Jenny,


stay the hell away from Fendi.


        Avoid the bench I've claimed
as my new country. Don't play
with me
        down in the dirt or you'll find shovelfuls
of pinworms up your skirt.


We're not lover/twins, Love-Hewett,
        not even friends.
                But I could be the orphan that you chose.
We'd laugh and eat together        like on the show.


—On set you'll share vacation pics of us
together on your phone.


I want to hear you say it:


                *without her I'd just be alone.*

the closest I'd get

    to the ocean


was by ferrying pilgrim

    bus passes,

        gum wrappers, scratched off

    lotto tickets

        to the storm

    drain

        with my piss.

           Want my advice?

Learn to spread your lips.

      Tilt your pelvis

    forward and with practice,


           stand up like a man.


Don't be mistaken


    for something sweet,

        feminine,


           full of holes.


41

## MOUSE.

We're huddled in the dark because the room's painted black,

    because the eyeless sister shook us
and foretold a helicopter circling the roof.

Any minute we'll be cornered.
    Any minute, men with guns will find us.

But we can hide here,

    our whispers coiling, watching
yellow stars writhe
        and scatter in our eyes.

The ceiling's wide hand flexes
    above us, almost

        infinite, suppressing our movement.

        And I want an excuse

to touch your lips

    but the air's equipped with little tongues.

The air has eaten our faces.

Mouse, it's always repeating itself:
　　　us in darkness, waiting for monsters who never come,

　　　waiting to be gutted, our insides slurped.


　　　　I can tell the story until it's a whimper

　　　　　　until we no longer exist.

*In this story, we kiss until the sun axes the walls.*
　　　　*In this story, the earth screams and thrashes beneath us.*
　*In this story, we crash through the floor and are absorbed.*

　　—But tell me how it ends.


Tell me this will end if we say it's over.

# THERE'S NO ONE DEFINING MOMENT THAT KILLS YOU

Two boys face off in a hallway: one holds a switchblade, one wields a boxcutter pulled from his boot. Each is capable of killing the other. Here comes tragedy, galloping like a rage-blind horse on fire.

In the story of Pocahontas, a girl stops death by placing her skull before the hammer. Mouse, I covered your heart with my own and closed my eyes.

I saved your life. Later, you opened your wrists in a bathtub.

Robby said someone would have died right then if I hadn't intervened. He named it courage, though he was mistaken. Under pressure, anyone accepts the call to act. The courageous can accept this will not make a goddamn difference.

*44*

## HOW TO REINTEGRATE INTO SOCIETY: A CHECKLIST

| | |
|---|---|
| Lie | ☑ |
| Lie about when you've lied | ☑ |
| Lie about what you've lied about | ☑ |
| Lie about being a bad liar | ☑ |
| Fabricate your home town your home | |
| state your home country | ☑ |
| Never share what books you've really read | ☑ |
| Example: *What's your alma mater?* | ☑ |
| Further Example: *Me too! Let's be friends* | ☑ |
| Advanced Example: *I love to lie* | ☑ |
| *in bed* ~~next to your unconscious body~~ | |
| ~~my own blank eyes open to the deep throated~~ | |
| ~~night trying to remember what name~~ | |
| ~~I wore for you~~ | |
| Lie by remaining compliant | ☑ |
| by remaining silent | ☑ |
| by feigning indifference | ☑ |
| Turn those lies into oil slick | |
| black boots and stomp stomp stomp | |
| out any trace of what you are | ☑ |
| Bury those embers in a pit of lies | |
| on a moonless beach of lies surrounded | |
| by a fleckless gulf of untruth | ☑ |
| Leave them to smolder | ☑ |

# MR. BLACK LOSES HIS SUBJECT (FOUND WADDED IN THE CORNER OF A TWEEKER SQUAT)

Don't you listen here shitkicker. I says. Put em down. Put each one to bed and shut the door. Let the demon skinhead kids alone. Leave em alone. I says. I ain't your day-room antennae rock n' roll man roofus. Shitkicker. I says. I ain't gonna post Annie Oakley's target dummies **feel** me to say. Or start a war with Tom Selleck to report your skinhead demon ass to the FBI. I says. I'll support you for de-por-ta-tion. I says. I'll send you right back **less** a leg shitlicker. To the FBI. I says. I ain't here to lick more flies off Tom Selleck tied down and **alone** for any demon wannabe. I says. Annie Oakley dummies tagging wifi spots for DE-POR-TA-TION. Straight to the EFF BEE AYE. SHITKICKER. I ain't **without** nobody's god. I says. I ain't a systematic, posttraumatic, autocratic, emblematic, transatlantic, raccoons in the attic, liar, cheat, or addict, slummer, gunner, bummer, no-brain zombie runner. I says. Listen. Don't go through with **you** just put the weapon down. Shitkicker. Don't start a war with Annie Oakley's post-production float. Don't puts the thought to me. I says. Don't plant no gun on me or dig your muddy seeds. I ain't a post-it note or hole. Shitlicker. Don't listen here. I says.

46

## CHERRY-BABY,

What was your mantra? *Sometimes*
*you've gotta suck a little cock to get what you want.*

When I say that now,
people look at me in revulsion.

No one understands better than you
that we're all whores at brass tacks. I try to remember where

I last saw your silhouette: was it robed
in sunlight, smiling on a pier? Even the ocean was greedy

for a fondle, and would have swallowed you whole
like an antipsychotic or heroin balloon.

Darling, lay back on the settee. Let the rabbit-fur collar
kiss your neck's stubbled skin. We'll redact

your lipstick, smudged, and bleeding
mascara. We'll redact your broken

heel. Have a petit-four and a cup of tea.
We'll talk men and pretend they've been civil.

*after the photograph, "Still Life With Real and Fake Lemons"*


I want to call it art:

        hopefully a definition gives it meaning.


                The background—clotted

watercolor lemons scrolled

        onto a mass-production vinyl curtain—keeps repeating

*cluster      cluster      cluster      cluster.*


Concealed beneath this metastatic dropcloth,

the table in the foreground may not even be a table;


        it could be a shelf for all I know, or worse,

a piece of plywood elevated by some cinderblocks.


        In the middle of it squats the pyramid

of yellow citrus, with impostors,

as a challenge.


I know this scene lies to me:  its creator says it right up front.

Some of what I see is real, some fake,

some scooped and sculpted out of porcelain,

glazed with toxic ink,

        some promise to render juice if squeezed.


*48*

Floodlights lobbing artificial sunshine suffocate

        all shape from my imaginary bounty.


Each piece, in hand, can't make the overwhelming whole.

      I need everything at once:

                those rows

repeating rows of endless fruit and trees.


Any sky, any trace of sanity,

      any exits must be spackled over.

we had words, Justice & Atrocity. We had words, candle & blanket.
When in need, writing *No Talent* on cardboard often earned enough
to feed us all. They laughed at our little chant on the corner,
singing *spare some change spare some change*, clanging our cans
just in time to catch their quarters. One foot orbiting around the
other; it takes skill to dance all fancy like a circus animal. Sitting
in the squat one night you said you didn't want dirty anymore.
You wanted a summer with a beautiful woman. You wanted a
table and chairs. It was the only time we spoke in such a fashion.
You'd been a medic in the war and knew how to keep the wound
from bleeding a person to death. *It's not about pressure*, you said,
*it's about convincing them they can live without the blood they've lost.*

You've become the poem.

> *Blood* shoulders *need* and *enough*

through the blazing

> trochees of your heart        [humming *mire mire mire mire*]

> > Tangled marquee titles scroll

> > > *injury* & *strength,*        *can't*

and *never.*


Your muscles' tense: *losing losing lost lost lost.*

Translucent space

> divides each     word     and letter;

 your body, the evidence, all ash.


This is the only way I can construct you anymore.

"If Ever Asked to Describe All It Was (Written on a Palimpsest of Truman Capote's *In Cold Blood*)"

Title inspired by Perry Smith's journal entry "If ever called upon to make a speech"

Original Paragraph from *In Cold Blood*
"Holcomb, too, can be seen from great distances. Not that there is much to see—simply an aimless congregation of buildings divided in the center by the main-line tracks of the Santa Fe Railway, a haphazard hamlet bounded on the south by a brown stretch of the Arkansas (pronounced "Ar-kan-sas") River, on the north by a highway, Route 50, and on the east and west by prairie lands and wheat fields. After rain, or when snowfalls thaw, the streets, unnamed, unshaded, unpaved, turn from the thickest dust into the direst mud. At one end of the town stands a stark old stucco structure, the roof of which supports an electric sign—"DANCE"—but the dancing has ceased and the advertisement has been dark for several years. Nearby is another building with an irrelevant sign, this one in flaking gold on a dirty window—"HOLCOMB BANK." The bank failed in 1933, and its former counting rooms have been converted into apartments. It is one of the town's two "apartment houses," the second being a ramshackle mansion known, because a good part of the local school's faculty lives there, as the Teacherage. But the majority of Holcomb's homes are one-story frame affairs, with front porches."

"A Week of Meals for Little Mohawked Squatter Punk:: Bingo Edition":
the bingo board outcome: "sleep for dinner" is taken from the title of the song "Sleep for Dinner" by the hip-hop group, Lords of the Underground

"Growing Up Is Losing Some Illusions, In Order to Acquire Others":
The title is a quote from Virginia Woolf

"How to Capture the Escaping Man"
after a photo in Larry Clark's "Tulsa"

"There's No One Defining Moment That Kills You"
the title is taken from a quote from the comedian, Sinbad "there's no one defining moment
that kills you or makes you"

"What Happened in Los Angeles"
after the photograph, "Still Life With Real and Fake Lemons" by Rachel Stern

# ACKNOWLEDGMENTS

Previous incarnations of pieces from this collection have appeared in *Salamander, Natural Bridge, Folio, Thumbnail Review, Painted Bride Quarterly, TNY Press' Electric Encyclopedia of Experimental Literature, The Fem, Barrelhouse, Forklift, Ohio,* & the chapbook *Zoo for Well-Groomed Eaters.*

Thank you to the amazing team at Yes Yes Books, and to my generous friends and mentors who lent their time and energy to this manuscript.

Thank you to Travis Ewell, who helped me to remember how it really happened. Rest in peace, buddy.

**LAUREN BRAZEAL** teaches in Dallas and is the author of two chapbooks, *Zoo for Well-Groomed Eaters* (Dancing Girl Press, 2016), and *exuviae* (Horse Less Press, 2016). Her first full-length collection, *Gutter*, released in 2018 from Yes Yes Books. In her past, Brazeal has been a homeless gutter-punk, a resident of Ecuador's Amazon jungle, a maid, a surfer chick, and a custom aquarium designer. A graduate of Bennington's MFA program in writing and literature, her work has appeared in journals such as *DIAGRAM*, *Smartish Pace*, *Barrelhouse*, *Forklift, Ohio*, and *Verse Daily*.

## Full-Length Collections

*i be, but i ain't* by Aziza Barnes

*The Feeder* by Jennifer Jackson Berry

*What Runs Over* by Kayleb Rae Candrilli

*Love the Stranger* by Jay Deshpande

*Blues Triumphant* by Jonterri Gadson

*North of Order* by Nicholas Gulig

*Meet Me Here at Dawn* by Sophie Klahr

*I Don't Mind If You're Feeling Alone* by Thomas Patrick Levy

*Sons of Achilles* by Nabila Lovelace

*Reaper's Milonga* by Lucian Mattison

*If I Should Say I Have Hope* by Lynn Melnick

*Landscape with Sex and Violence* by Lynn Melnick

*GOOD MORNING AMERICA I AM HUNGRY AND ON FIRE* by jamie mortara

*some planet* by jamie mortara

*Boyishly* by Tanya Olson

*Pelican* by Emily O'Neill

*The Youngest Butcher in Illinois* by Robert Ostrom

*A New Language for Falling Out of Love* by Meghan Privitello

*I'm So Fine: A List of Famous Men & What I Had On* by Khadijah Queen

*American Barricade* by Danniel Schoonebeek

*The Anatomist* by Taryn Schwilling

*Gilt* by Raena Shirali

*Panic Attack, USA* by Nate Slawson

*[ insert ] boy* by Danez Smith

*Man vs Sky* by Corey Zeller

*The Bones of Us* by J. Bradley

  [ Art by Adam Scott Mazer ]


## Chapbook Collections

### VINYL 45S

*After* by Fatimah Asghar

*Inside My Electric City* by Caylin Capra-Thomas

*Dream with a Glass Chamber* by Aricka Foreman

*Pepper Girl* by Jonterri Gadson

*Of Darkness and Tumbling* by Mónica Gomery

*Bad Star* by Rebecca Hazelton

*Makeshift Cathedral* by Peter LaBerge

*Still, the Shore* by Keith Leonard

*Please Don't Leave Me Scarlett Johansson* by Thomas Patrick Levy

*Juned* by Jenn Marie Nunes

*A History of Flamboyance* by Justin Phillip Reed

*No* by Ocean Vuong

*This American Ghost* by Michael Wasson


### BLUE NOTE EDITIONS

*Beastgirl & Other Origin Myths* by Elizabeth Acevedo

*Kissing Caskets* by Mahogany L. Browne

*One Above One Below: Positions & Lamentations* by Gala Mukomolova


### COMPANION SERIES

*Inadequate Grave* by Brandon Courtney

*The Rest of the Body* by Jay Deshpande